MW01602320

Cutting Edge

OTHER BOOKS by Bernhard Hillila –

Poetry:
a fly on the swatter
The Haven: New Poetry
Prose:
The Sauna Is . . .
History of the Indiana-Kentucky Synod,
Lutheran Church in America 1970-1987
Translations:
(from the Finnish of Olavi Kaukola)
Riches of Prayer
About Time to Pray

CUTTING EDGE

Poems by

BERNHARD HILLILA

Chimney Hill Press

Some of these poems appeared originally in:
The Formalist, The Cresset, The Lyric, Soundings, Skylark, Potpourri, Hopewell Review, The Haven, and *The Boston University Alumni Poetry Center Journal.*

Cover design: Richard H. W. Brauer

Cover art: *Cradling Wheat,* 1939, lithograph
Thomas Hart Benton, American (1889-1975)
courtesy Valparaiso University Museum of Art
photographed by Richard H. W. Brauer and Jack A. Hiller

First Edition
Library of Congress Catalog Card Number: 95-71935
ISBN: 0-9627300-2-5

Printed in the United States of America by
Western Newspaper Publishing Co., Inc.
Indianapolis, IN

To

Es, Chris, and Marty

ABOUT THE AUTHOR

Bernhard Hillila is a graduate of Boston University (A.B. in philosophy), Lutheran School of Theology in Chicago (theology), Case-Western University (M.A. in psychology), and Columbia University (Ed.D. in educational administration). As a Lutheran pastor, he had parishes in Massachusetts, New York City, and Ohio. Currently Professor Emeritus of Education at Valparaiso University, he earlier served Suomi College and Theological Seminary as president, Wittenberg University as seminary dean and director of graduate studies, and California Lutheran University as dean of the faculty. Hillila currently devotes much of his time to poetry: writing, lecturing, judging contests, conducting workshops, and giving readings. He is listed in *Who's Who in America*.

THANKS

I give thanks to my wife Esther for both poetic inspiration and helpful critique; to our children – Esther, Christine, and Martin – for their continuing interest in what their dad is writing; and to Ed Byrne for mentoring me in poetry.

I express special thanks to Jack Hiller of Chimney Hill Press for nudging me into gathering these poems and thus making the publication of this book possible.

– Bernhard Hillila

PREFACE

It will be good news to Bernie Hillila's readers that, after several years of publishing in the poetry journals, he has come out with another book. Those of us who admire him in all his admirable ways are glad once again to engage his wit, wisdom and sensitivity. Within these pages, as always, Bernie demonstrates (to borrow an expression from Laurens van der Post) "that capacity for *participation mystique* in the world around him" that to me is the mark of the true poet. He reveals and we see.

Robert Frost once said that the poet is entitled to anything the reader finds in his poems. We, Bernie's readers, wish that we could feel entitled to (i. e., deserving of) what we find in his poems. Entitled or not, we are beneficiaries of his gifts.

To those of you who are new readers of Bernie's poetry: Welcome!

– Jack A. Hiller

CONTENTS

I From "Master Weaver"
to "True Believer"

II From "Lullabye"
to "Awakenings"

III From "Learning to Speak"
to "Just Say 'No!'"

I

From "MASTER WEAVER"

to "TRUE BELIEVER"

MASTER WEAVER

Old master weaver Omar was in charge
of each detail: "These leaves of indigo
make perfect blue." His mind had spun the large
design that balanced color shades just so.
He supervised the shearing, checked the heft
of new-spun yarn. Each hour he walked around
the loom where weavers interlaced soft weft
through warp with skill that made Sarouk renowned.
Where Mecca-pointing arrows clustered, he
had crafted in a small mistake, just one.
"Since only Allah can be perfect, we
cannot present as flawless what we've done!"
    He sold his long-worked carpet cheap, because
    his wife discovered seven other flaws.

SOLO PIECE

In the hush of Orchestra Hall
Luigi feels accelerando
in the beat of his heart,
crescendo in his veins.

His solo is the evening's first,
and though he's played it countless
times, it's still the most
demanding in all his repertoire.

As mind and ears rehearse the clean
sforzando attack over and over,
he dries his hands once more,
moistens and purses his lips.

At last he gets his nod
and to the expectant audience
of orchestra blows Absolute Truth –
the oboe's definitive "A."

CUTTING EDGE

A blade has cut the ground plow-deep. Earth lies
spread open, waiting seed and spring's surprise.
    In deep-waled corduroy, Ed's fields stretch past
    the pond and far beyond to Nelsons' grassed
front yard where double rows of poplars rise.
       *   *   *
Ed weighs his sale to Merchants' Mall – the "why's"
of money, health and age. Between his sighs
    he hears the reaper where, with diesel blast,
        a blade has cut the ground.
       *   *   *
Ed's family and his neighbors dry their eyes
as they hear Pastor Keller eulogize
    old Ed, how he was faithful to the last
hard, wheezing breath. They know: beyond the massed
bouquets, beneath the plastic sod's disguise,
        a blade has cut the ground.

ANDREW

Andrew covered the roses,
brought in the zucchini,
reflecting that he had so little
to do and so much time to do it.

Andrew was a grey-hearted man
pulled down by his own suspenders.
A fogey since he'd been a teen-ager,
he'd had a half-life of 70 years —
he'd fought the wrong war, taken
the wrong job, married Margaret.
With never anything to celebrate,
he seldom smiled, never laughed.

He did feel deeply about some things,
like Chevys changing the controls
for wipers from left to right.
And he still was sore that in '93
he'd given $10 to "Feed the Poor,"
a gift that wasn't tax deductible.

He'd never bought anything on impulse,
and what he bought was bottom-drawer.
Yet everything he owned was organized:
bills in his wallet, 1's through 20's
heads up and cleanest to the front;
all the clocks in his clapboard house
synchronized to the minute.

Andrew had a good side, which didn't
show in photos: he loved his brothers --
both of them -- as much as he was able.
He mowed his own lawn, fixed his own
car, made love to his own wife.
And he didn't fart loudly even when
watching TV alone in his own bedroom.
He bored Father Kelly at confession.

Wide-tied but narrow-souled,
he glimpsed the mountains to the west,
but he'd never wanted to climb one.
Nor did he wonder what might be
beyond.

WILFRED

A spare, angular man from a square flat state,
Wilfred wore both belt and suspenders,
sported a "Co-op" cap to high school games
and to mid-morning coffee at the Big Wheel.
He was a red-meat-and-potatoes man,
taking his meals at 8 a.m., noon, and 6 p.m.
and checking the outcome of bowel movements.
Since the bottle for his procardia said, "Do not
drink alcohol when taking this medication,"
he took no pills when drinking neat whiskey.

End feather in the right wing of Gingrich's Old Party,
Wilfred listened to Louis Rukeyser, Lawrence Welk
and Rush Limbaugh, read *Reader's Digest*
and newspaper columnists who agreed with him.
Once in a while, he went to a Moose Hall dance,
in his pocket a condom he'd bought years ago,
just in case. On some Wednesday nights he'd play
pinochle at the Lodge, but he never gambled.

Wilfred's faith was a stand, not a leap.
Every Sunday he went to Bible Baptist Church,
where he'd tried for choir. found he was a monotone.
Almost as a ritual, after church, he visited
Evergreen Cemetery, where he'd placed a stone
with "Astrid Swenson" to mark his mother's grave –
a lesser stone awaited "Wilfred Swenson."

His clean apartment, sparsely furnished in motley
garage sale and Grandma Moses, was secured
by locks, deadbolts, and smoke alarms. He'd willed
his apartment, Olds, bonds, and stamp collection
to his half-sister Emily's kids, with a generous
bequest to his church. He added codicils often.

Wilfred's latest Olds had seat belts, of course, plus
"The Club," anti-lock brakes and dual airbags,
although he always drove alone. He almost never
traveled by plane; when General Engineering insisted
he fly to Cleveland, he'd buy extra trip insurance.

After all, Wilfred didn't want his life to end
the way it had begun – by accident.

PENTECOST 1993 IN CHICAGO

In this chill Windy City once reborn
through fire, Brother Ed, a flaming preacher
with flaring megaphone in hand, rages
on at State and Randolph, warning
heedless throngs with a hand-lettered sign:
"The LORD your GOD is a consuming FIRE!"

With hot eyes, blistering tongue, Ed fulminates
about the winds of passion, fires of war,
and proves the brimstone end is near.
Undaunted by the fire-resistant souls that pass
him by, incendiary Ed urges wayward
shoppers to repent while there is time.

Across the street, Louie listens but suspects
the Lord is not to be found in these searing
fires, these tornadic winds. With still,
small voice, he coaxes homeless Crazy Harry
down the sidewalk to McDonald's.

A pigeon bows its iridescent neck
toward the feet of the prophet, Brother Ed.

TERESA

Teresa was the one who showed me how
to swing. She listened to my blandishing,
and that's as much as I can tell you now.

We'd build our castles in the sand as though
we built them in the air, where, on the wing,
Teresa was. The one who showed me how

to pick ripe cherries from the bending bough?
Teresa, who delighted in her fling –
and that's as much as I can tell. You know,

I hadn't known how girls could gleam and glow
until with her I knew awakening –
Teresa was the one. Who showed me how

to love another human being? Oh,
my own Teresa's spark lit everything,
and that's as much as I can tell you now.

Today, before my God I'll make my vow
and offer her a golden wedding ring.
Teresa was the one who showed me how,
and that's as much as I can tell you now.

OSCAR

After Annie died in January, Oscar
couldn't stand the empty town anymore.

One Thursday, after shoveling the walk,
still getting to work ten minutes early,
he quit his job at the Co-op just like that.

He said he couldn't stand the cold anymore.
He wrote down half a dozen names
of people who promised references
"any time you need one, any time."

Oscar sold his house to Juan from Dallas,
who'd come to computerize the Waterworks,
who'd been looking for a house for months
while staying with Maria at the Super 8.

Oscar auctioned much of the furniture,
sent Annie's clothes to his sister Irene,
donated his snowmobile to the Ski Club,
threw away eight cartons of junk.

So his walls and table-top would be familiar,
he took the silver, glassware, dishes --
even the chipped set of Desert Rose --
and all the pictures from the walls except
the landscape Annie's sister had done.

All that, plus the rocker and Lazy Boy,
the VCR and TV, the toaster and stereo,
four boxes of papers and photos, even
the double bed, fit into one 4 x 8 U-Haul.

Oscar said goodbyes to the good guys
on the Norsemen Curling Team at Tony's,
where they'd all gone after beating
the Iroquois 5-3. He wished them the best.
They wished him the best, shook his hand,
and after he'd left, they shook their heads.

He gave farewell handshakes to the Tollefsens
and the Koskis, neighbors right and left, who
worried about "the changing neighborhood."

      *   *   *   *

Having left a state that produced iron,
wheat and lumber for one that majored
in whiskey, tobacco and race horses,

Oscar rented a walk-up apartment,
bought some new used furniture,
stocked the freezer and the fridge.

On his third try, following up on ads
in *The Sentinel*, Oscar got a job
as salesman at Goodrich Tires.

Raised a Methodist, then "born again,"
he now attended St. Thomas Episcopal.
He joined its "Toms" bowling team,
went to greyhound races on Fridays.

Having grown up on oatmeal and cornflakes,
Oscar tried fried mush and grits.
Not seeing pike or walleye on the menu,
he ordered fried catfish and okra.

He dated Lucy, a hostess at Shoney's,
for over a month and met her family.

And then, one Thursday, after reading
The Sentinel over coffee and doughnuts,
still getting to work a half-hour early,
he quit his job at Goodrich just like that
and went back home to Bemidji, Minnesota.

14

SETH

And Adam knew his wife again, and she bore a son and called his name Seth.

His scant obituary noted: "Seth,
third son of Adam, patriarch of the clan –
his brothers both preceded him in death;
a host of children mourn the man."

Who can forget young, martyred Abel? Who
does not remember sibling rival Cain
in exile, forehead marked with God's tattoo
and hands forever blotched with bloody stain?

Engrossed in hero or in villain, we
forget the common Seth, replacement for
slain Abel. Average, undistinguished, he
leads us to David, Jesus – many more!

Seth surely is the patron saint of all
unnoticed saints whose lives are written small.

NARROW DOORS

A narrow door stands at the mother-end
of each small life, a threshold that must send
new-borns to venture – womb to breast to knee,
then later on, from apron strings cut free,
out to the vast world, where each alone must fend.

When Jesus asked re-birth of an old friend,
the thought made Nicodemus' logic bend
and break: must entry to God's kingdom be
        a narrow door?

Confronted by constraints, our strong wills tend
to smash all narrow portals and to rend
each bar, break locks for which we find no key.
Frustrated by life's limits, finally
we see wide-open at life's other end
        a narrow door.

LIFE HAS NO GUARANTEES

What we so
          dearly treasure has been got
most times with talent, time and sweat, or fought
     for, hoping heirs would benefit, their ship
     come in. And yet, the price of stocks may dip
to nil and gold not hold the shine we'd thought.

What we so
          often as a prize have sought
is prone to sloth and moth, can rust and rot –
     we re-set goals and oftentimes must rip
          what we sew.

What we so
          value-consciously have bought
may prove to be a hook on which we're caught
     as losers in some scam or devious gyp.
     But then again, an over-generous tip
and unearned grace prove we don't always reap
          what we sow.

COUNTDOWN

When Harry's kids once asked, "What
would Dad like for Father's Day?"
Millie had answered, "He could use a new
Rolfs cowhide extra-large keyholder."

Harry'd carried Security Trust keys
for his office, his desk, his filing
cabinets, and for the executive washroom.

Years ago, before he really understood
what doors his choices had locked for him,
there'd even been a key to Sue's apartment
in a hidden flap behind the other keys.
For years he'd needed keys for two cars.

Then, when Millie died, he gave the Honda
keys to Joe. Failing his driver's test
after sixty years of driving, he parted
with the Olds and its keys for $5,000.

That year the kids convinced him
that the house was "just too much."
He placed it on the market with the keys
to doors, to deadbolts, to the garage.

Since emphysema didn't travel well, Harry
put the Tourister keys in the closet
with the luggage. He put his safe-deposit
key in the roll-top with his will.

Coming home to Apartment B-4 last night,
he'd just taken out the key ring
with the blue plastic "Investors Mutual"
tag — and its one key.

LOVE REMAINS

"And as they dug, they found
the skeletons of a man and a
woman who evidently had been
buried alive in an embrace."

Interred without coroner's autopsy,
mortician's mortuary art,
buried without priest, flowers or funeral,
entombed without eulogy
in unhallowed ground –
the owners of these bones are gone.

The "I'll-be-damned!" bulldozer operator,
the impatient real estate developer,
the morbidly fascinated gapers-by
can speed read basic body language
of devotion, of vows held far beyond
"till death do us part."

That hidden hug enjoyed
longer than living lovers could wish
surpasses by years "the longest kiss"
in *Guinness' Book of Records.*

20

Embracing bare but without breasts,
kissing stripped but without lips
make heatless passion in unfeeling dust.
Cold shoulders give cold comfort
to skinless cheeks.

And yet these fossil bones,
in the coupling anatomy of love –
pallid mandible to clavicle,
pale carpals to scapula,
ashen tibia to fibula,
wan ilium to sacrum –
provide post-morten evidence
of love that will not let love go.

THE TRUE BELIEVER

Across from Fidelity Bank and Trust's
pillared facade on which someone
had spray-painted "Trust Jesus,"
gullible Theodore Glauber,
a recovering agnostic,
gulped down his fourth Heileman's
("a beer you can believe in")
to strains of Sean Cassidy's
"Do you believe in magic?"

One of the faithful,
he was brass-railing
in Broken Promises Bar
where "Keep the faith, Baby!"
was magic-markered above the urinal
and where fatherly Phil
the Bartender heard confessions.

Ted offered his Master Card
with complete confidence,
relying on plastic credit –
not needing any denomination
of "In-God-We-Trust" paper.

II

From "LULLABYE"

to "AWAKENINGS"

LULLABYE

Bye-a-lulla,
bye-a-lulloo.
I am your mother,
I'll rock you to sleep.

Bye-a-lulla,
bye-a-lulloo.
I love your father –
his love too runs deep.

Bye-a-lulla,
bye-a-lulloo.
You're flesh of my flesh,
our blood bonds will keep.

Bye-a-lulla,
bye-a-lulloo.
I count the long months –
your life is not cheap.

Bye-a-lulla,
bye-a-lulloo.
After you're born, I'll
still rock you to sleep.

REFLECTIONS

A flare of flitting minnows swirls
through golden willow branches chasing
silver shivers of a liquid sun.

Hewn from shimmered cumulus, a palace
floats halfway between my beach and me,
bobs through hanging-garden lily pads.

West winds ruffle rushes growing
from green-lichened granite, ripple
bluish granite likeness in the lake.

Silently my rowboat slices through
a dock that's slivered by sheer water.
My pleated image undulates
upon the pond's accordion waves.

ANGELS ARE THE FIRST TO KNOW

Last year, 1,000 western yellow-billed
cuckoos, love-nesting in California
cottonwoods and willows, lost their
songs to polluted air.

Yeah, a bird –
I used to work with a bird.
I owe my life to a bird!

When I was an achiever under
ground digging black diamond
in Susquehanna Number Three,
our crew had four men and one canary.

Before we'd start our shift,
we'd check in at the change house
and pick up our "Angel."
Nick, the crew boss, used to tease
our bird with his black humor,
"Come on, Angel, go to hell with us!"

Whichever bird we happened to get,
her name was always "Angel" –
the whole sacrificial flock christened
by some dusty, long-gone miner.

Yeah, the canaries had bright wings,
sang songs, looked heavenly –
but that's not why they got their name.
It was "Angel" as in "guardian angel."
Each one-ounce savior kept watch
over muscled men with lives at risk.

Chirping in the sunless underground,
poor Angel seldom saw the heavens!
The tunnel was more like Purgatory,
a black hole for a dark business.
The carbide lanterns on our caps
were eerie headlights, as we did
a night's work even on the day shift.
The mine was a somber cover over us
men and over our bird in her little cage.

Angel's cage had some canary seed,
a bit of water; and at lunchtime,
when steel no longer grated on rock,
some smudge-lipped guy might give her
a crumb of bread, a shred of lettuce.

We men and our canary lived
in an ebony mix of trees and ferns

from when Earth was fresh as Eden.
We worked in cemeteries of buried
plants, acres of stored black sunshine.

Blasting, picking, shoveling, laying track,
loading cars to send to the tipple, we spent
our energy in grubbing out the raw energy
of rough rock. We practiced our black art,
mined the black, powered mineral which,
unleashed, would heat company houses,
release live steam for turbines, create
sheet steel, and through its black magic
would give aspirins for aching heads,
nylons for shapely legs, lavender dye
for silk dresses, cologne for soft necks.

As our crew worked the mine face,
down a drift along a bituminous seam,
coal dust clung to clothes and bodies –
black faces, black hands, black lungs.
Only the blackdamp was colorless.

Then, one dreary Monday morning,
in the middle of some heavy shoveling,
Mulrooney yelled, "Angel's down!"

And down she was, limp and songless,
legs and toes curled like calligraphy,
glassy eyes open to black death.
All of that we got in one glance
before we rushed headlong in panic
to the shaft, as we'd been drilled –
abandoning car and picks and leaving
one little bird on an unlit altar.

OCTOBER

October blowing
flocks of starlings, maple leaves,
one Campbell plaid skirt.

Over gold aspens
two clouds nearing each other –
a lone thrush's call.

Technicolor leaves –
ten grackles rabble-rousing
under gravestone skies.

The hawk's left wing dips,
a shadow sweeps the high weeds –
sumacs burn to death.

The far sun reaching
through the musk of fallen leaves –
feathers winging south.

Now we see the nest,
as red-breasted leaves fly down –
only the wind sings.

INDIANA DUNES

This is where, 12,000 years ago,
the glacier wept farewell
and left the Lake for us.
This is where for centuries
the winds have built the Dunes –
where pioneering marram grass
and early sand cherry anchored
blowing grains of quartz
to mounds, foredunes, high hills.
Between the yin and yang
of lake and land,
the magic of the shore erupts.
Separated long ago,
dry land and water ever lust
for one another.

The lake threatens as it blesses –
erodes, yet nourishes.
Streams bring tons of flecks,
vapor floats toward the sky,
and rains splash down to earth,
recycling one primordial water.

Here Sandburg thanked "for art
and pause." Here Dudley painted
thousands of the dunes' nuances.
Here we build our castles in the sand.

We come to focus eyes beyond our walls,
soak and sun our skins,
stretch our legs cross-country
and our arms from hang gliders.

We stretch our minds in meditation here
where the dunes move and the sands sing,
where our thoughts move
over the face of the waters
and the skin of the land.

FLIGHT OF FANCY

The sacred secret of flight
is in wishbones, not wings;
not in jet roar, but dreams
that soar as an angel swings.

Ask eaglets daring to lunge,
or Orville and Wilbur who
finally got it right –
and check Apollo 2.

Yet dreams need wakenings
and wings must fold to fact.
Ask Icarus, who fell
from his high-flier act.

NEAR TATEYAMA

1. The Bay
We hear
the susurrus
of sirens and sea grass
and see the cool foam of cirrus
above.

2. The Mountain
Beyond
the cherry branch
with its wild eruption,
old snow-headed Fuji rises
the same.

3. The Magician
West winds
pull a rabbit
out of a white-cloud hat
that was a dragon a moment
ago.

4. The Butterfly
Quickly
the swallows dart
past the chrysanthemum
throne on which one fragile Monarch
sits still.

FLORIDA KEYS

Florida ends engulfed in Gulf,
where it strews its last drop of land.
Skeleton keys open to its
last strand of strand.

Water makes the land rejoice,
but water from the land – from lot
and laundry, truck, and toilet – breaks
the ocean's heart.

Salty as tears, sour as urine,
the sea has rot upon its breath.
Algae are unraveling
the knot of death.

The echo system of each conch shell
sounds in the sea turtle's nest,
the sponge's thirst, the shark's ebbing
plankton-fest.

Ancient coral beds are prey
to rusty freighters, pleasure yachters,
while well-fed land developers
spoil their daughters.

There is no Ark to save the creatures
killed in floods that drown sea waters.

FULL OF THE PAST, FULL OF THE FUTURE

A leatherneck sea turtle beaches
herself on Florida's Jupiter Island,
lumbering ashore to nest, as she did
three years ago. A migrant survivor
who never knew her mother, she knows
the whens and wheres of turtle mothering.

This air-breathing reptile who lives
like a fish has flown underwater
like a big bird in slow motion, diving
half a mile to feast on jellyfish. Now
three thousand miles from her feeding
grounds, she surfaces from the sea
to nest and lay her eggs on land.

Here on the beach, this living fossil
is out of her element, an awkward alien
trapped by a ton of size and slowed
to a crawl by her armor, burdened
in the skeleton that is her closet.

But her digging now is dazzlingly fast,
a frantic whirlwind of sand. And then
the "klok," "klok" of eggs dropping —
over a hundred eggs in a clutch.
(There is strength in numbers buried.)

Suddenly she heads for salt water
without a backward glance, trusting
her eggs to a world of seagulls, raccoons,
poachers and beachfront builders.
She leaves for the safety of a sea
full of fishlines and shrimp nets.

ON OBSERVING A SUPERNOVA

For Stephen W. Hawking

Between the "naked singularities" of creative
Big Bang
     and collapsing black hole crunch,
we curious children ask if time began
     and when it ends.
Equidistant from our stars and atoms, we ask
what matter is, why it started,
          when it ends –
     what it all matters.

Even with Hubble, how can we understand
the scope and underlying order of the galaxies
     in our expanding universe?
Why are so many of our questions
answered with more questions?
          "And why not?"
With Heisenberg, we grow more certain
     of uncertainty.
    *   *   *   *

Wheelchair-trapped for twenty years,
you travel space by force of thought
from just a millionth-millionth of an inch
     to a million million million million miles.

Lou Gehrig of our day, you hit
upon some new hypothesis, then run
computer programs to communicate, catch
             our attention with synthetic speech.

Staring down deep space, you ponder
white dwarf stars, "quasars with red shifts,"
"black holes with no hair,"

                         pulsars pulsing,
You ride the arrows of time through time,
think the thoughts of God

                    through space.

Probing atoms past protons and neutrons,
you're charmed by strange Joycean quarks
             in six "flavors," each in three "colors,"
by "antiquarks, gluons and glueballs,"
by the deviant spins of wave particles.
Electromagnetic and nuclear forces
             are with you always.

In our relentless search to see as one
             and whole our maze of universe,
which "goes to all the trouble of existing,"
yet keeps so many secrets, you blow
             our minds past space/time's warp.

GONE FISHING

On the dog-day lake
still oars rest in their oarlocks –
a four-o'clock moon.

In front of the boat
a school of minnows glinting
through willow shadows.

The lake has wrinkled
in pickerel-sized circles –
horseflies buzz the shore.

One arc of nylon
from fishing rod to fish jaw –
a splash of water.

In the boat's shadow,
silver bodies on a string
near a cool six-pack.

SQUID

The body pulses,
ten sinuous arms cascade –
Shiva of the sea.

High-lighted eyes stare
as the gray body transmutes –
cascades of color.

Disappearaing act?
No – a sea chameleon's
private camouflage.

Black-cape magician
jets quickly under cover
of its own ink screen.

SPLASH

1

The rivulet
          splashes
                    down
washes
          down
     splash-carved
          time-carved
                    canyons

skipping
          stone to
                    stone to
     the water's
                    edge.

2

At   the water's
                    edge
a ten-year-old
                in stone-
washed
    blue-jeans
            swings his arm
back

skipping
        stones
            splashing
                stones
from wave
        to wave to
                wave.

THE SNAG*

The snag on his back acres bothered Mort.

The varied trees which lumbermen had killed
to frame the quaint Cape Codder he had bought
or to provide his Governor Winthrop desk
or to panel the corporate Beacon Hill office –
those were filling their intended callings.
But here a long-dead tree was an affront.

An efficiency expert – one who trimmed dead
wood from product lines, production lines –
Mort wondered why this tree, dead for years,
was still allowed to stand among the living,
a skeleton from the previous owner's closet.
Mort would have his woods alive.

He did a casual, unsuccessful autopsy
for cause of death. Disease? Insects?
Just old age? Nor could he trace the family
of a tree so skinless, so dismembered.

(Yet, even when the wind blows, even when
the bough breaks, not all falls down. . . .)

Near the top, a yellow-shafted flicker darted
to its hole, perhaps to feed its babies
with termites found in the tree's debris
and plucked from the longhouse they had eaten
through sapwood under sloughing bark.

In its detritus of duff, what legacy
might this ancestral tree have hoarded
on or under ground in moss and lichen?
A curse of fungus for the forest?
Or a fund of nurture for a tumult of life?
A habitat for a community of raccoons?
A pasture for a colony of lizards?
A mine for a company of moles?

As he glimpsed a scurrying squirrel,
Mort's quickened thoughts revolved
around the forest recycling itself
in a food chain, in a wood chain
of hardwood to humus and back again.

He found it hard to place the time of death.

----

* A standing dead tree

AWAKENINGS

The anxious world yearns for awakenings
in seeds, in atoms. Lovers' hearts well know
the gift of soaring waiting in the wings.

Since Eden's womb, each garden, sun-stirred, springs
from sleep. Like love, which waits love's grace to grow,
the anxious world yearns for awakenings.

The hungry eaglet from its aerie soars
because God gave its genes, all time ago,
the gift of soaring. Waiting in the wings

of chance, each egg-ward wriggling sperm can bring
re-kindled hope, perhaps the embryo
the anxious world yearns for. Awakenings

are proper work for Muses who make Mings
from pestled clay, give dormant words a glow,
the gift of soaring waiting in the wings.

Even as the evening curfew rings
too soon, and Stygian waters swirl below,
the anxious world yearns for awakenings –
the gift of soaring waiting in the wings.

III

From "LEARNING TO SPEAK"

to "JUST SAY 'NO!'"

LEARNING TO SPEAK

From primal scream to car-phoned message
      E-mailed or faxed to answering machine,
we seek the gift of tongue, spewing out sounds
      in the spanking-new wail of a newborn,
in baby-talk and babble, in slurring, mumbling,
      muttering, or whispering sweet nothings,
yelling some things, crying out in monolog, talking
      back in dialog, committing abuse or helping
to wholeness in daily verbal give and take, shifting
      from dialect and accent to standard English,
translating other mother tongues and multi-lingual
      body language, lecturing, sermonizing,
swearing testimony, arguing philosophy, discussing
      heart-to-heart, and finding even in our last
words rasped on a deathbed, how hard it is to say
      "I'm sorry!"

INFORMATION BY-WAY

1

While at
his Pentium,
Joe read of Acme's deal,
stored memos on his laptop, left
for home.

2

Aboard
his five-fifteen,
Joe phoned his boss, Armand,
who took the call while driving his
Grand Am.

3

Armand,
on Highway Five,
relayed the news to his
home office, left a message on
E-mail.

4

Marie,
doing overtime,
knew news like that would be
of interest to her boss, sent Joan
a fax.

5

At home
with Prodigy,
Joan checked the Acme files,
set up a conference call for ten
a.m.

CONCRETE

When Springfield's Union St.
sidewalk was laid in '65,
SALLY AND DAVE
cemented their love
in the first of endless
squares east of Division.

Summer suns blistered,
late-fall ice storms glazed,
winter frosts heaved;
hand-in-handers strolled,
joggers labored,
strangers trampled
over private commitments
on that public walk.

Then, 30 years later,
inscriptions skewed and cracked,
jackhammers, not caring
what's in a name, undid
those concrete vows to rubble.

THE BENCH

I leaned up the rise, strode around
the bend and saw it sitting there –
a weathered wooden seat, the only
bench I'd seen along long miles.

To have it there made hikers' sense –
halfway into the rugged path,
it gave the legs a rest, the lungs
a breather on Trail Five's climb.

Embarrassed I had not pushed on,
I sat on the bench's lap and saw
a view I'd otherwise have missed –
the vista north, framed by trunks

and branches of old oaks. I saw
an Appalachian notch which let
the sky creep down the mountainsides.
Nearby, on his bent-twig bench, a sparrow

focused on a single leaf,
seeing something I could not.
My perch was clearly built to last,
with graying two-by-sixes bolted

into strong steel framing, resting
on legs rough-sawn from four-inch trunks.
Although the path was single file,
the bench was wide enough for two.

Stretching my arm along the back,
I found my fingers on initials
mated years ago. Could KT

and JD be still as close . . . ?

WITHOUT YOU

I'm half of a pair of scissors
just one half a pair o' dice
one sock in my washer
one leg of worn jeans
one voice of a duet
one hand clapping
one wing beating
one oar rowing
one loneone
just one
half
!

CONTINENTAL DIVIDE

On top of the world, up closest to the sun,
blown snowflakes fall on snow, destined to race
toward the east or – one inch left – to dash
far west. Some yearn to see Atlantic dawn,
some dream Pacific sunset. All will run
past gold-rush aspen, curmudgeon pine, then chase
the flecks of golden sun down rapids, splash
through miles of unspoiled gorges just for fun.

We're up nine thousand feet, yet far below
the snow-topped peak in lounge-car ease. We two,
aglow with tequila sunrise brightness, rest.
We yawn to clear our ears, ignore the view
of Moffat Tunnel's viscera that show
but dim through light-flocked glass. We both flow west.

MORT

Seated at his walnut desk
in the den, with its green grass
cloth and golden oak trim, Mort
looked out of the window in disgust
at Tabby who'd just caught a mouse:
"I really can't stand the sight
of anything dead!"

Dressed in a plaid wool shirt,
cotton slacks and cowhide shoes
to sup on pickled herring, ribs,
squash, and six-grain bread, Mort
wrinkled his nose at Jimmy showing
off a Monarch butterfly he'd found:
"You know I hate the sight
of anything dead!"

Interrupting his caressing
of the mahogany piano's ivories,
Mort looked at Miranda, pleasing
in her indigo silk gown, gave her
some twenties from his calfskin wallet:

"Why don't you have Jane get chablis
and escargots for Saturday? And how
about fresh flowers for the living
room's coral vase? I hate the sight
of anything dead!"

GEORGE DICHTER

After all, he'd been productive.
Three children, seven grandchildren.
Up to 30,000 bushels of hybrid corn
and 150 Landrace hogs a year.
Over 300 poems written during winters.

Besides, George mused with a wry smile,
there had been the inevitable by-products.
Enough dandruff to cover the Rushmore heads,
fingernails to scratch a grand canyon,
sewage to fill three gymnasiums
on a presidential campaign trail.

Finally, he'd leave less than
a bushel of Indiana topsoil where
the seed of his clan was sown.

George hoped others would like
the grandchildren, perhaps the poems.

FLIES IN UARDERE*

Negash,* barely four, can't feel the flies
that walk around his vacant eyes.
He does not see the wasted men from his
own village digging one more grave.
    Sihine* waves a hand across her last
    son's face to brush off memories
    of civil war, of hopes all turned to aches,
    of two weeks' walking in the sun.

His breath too shallow to disturb the flies
around his empty mouth, mute lips,
limp Negash, past expecting, simply waits
for anything to end the wait.
    Before the city of a thousand tents,
    a Belgian doctor sighs and gives
    the crew from CNN his estimates
    of refugees he fears he'll lose.

Fevered Negash does not stir the wisp
of blanket in Sihine's lap.
His syncopated heart still taps out muted
drumbeats against the meager ribs.
    The camp director, on network interview,
    cites broken trucks, impassable roads
    and graft. He'd hoped the planes would fly
    him milk instead of TV cameras.

A silver cross above her shriveled breasts,
Sihine whispers grace in soft Amharic,
offers Negash a dab of boiled wheat paste—
the porridge lingers on his tongue.
    Safe in the First World, the U.N. meets,
    discusses causes of death in the Third.

*   U-är´dĕ-rĕ, Nĕ´găsh, Sĭ-hē´nĭ

EMBODIMENT

Mario had overseen the constant mixing
of cement for much of new Saint Mary's –
molded sections of the flying buttresses,
saintly statues, grimacing gargoyles.

He wished Maria could have seen the building
finished; she'd lost her fight against
metastasizing cancer in her breast
just months before the church's dedication.

Now Mario stood stooped, reflective,
feeling her presence in that sacred place.
His rough right hand caressed the rounded
surface of a pillar in the chancel,

and he sighed a smile. In spite of Father John
and her family, she had asked to be cremated –
her fair but fragile flesh returned at last
to ash. To concrete-colored ash.

THE PSYCHE

1. Outlook

Her sky
is so narrow –
just a slice of gray fog
seen through her one dirty, narrow
window.

2. Needs

She kneads
warm, yeasty dough
with forceful fingers, fists,
as hidden anger finds release
she needs.

3. Dreams

Sound sleep,
midwife to dreams,
gives birth to darkling lusts,
casts them on the hidden stream still
flowing.

4. Memories

Longer
than the trip back
to pots, clocks, books, and bills,
memories of anemones
linger.

ON THE SHORE

You stood
        on the shore
    reflected
    perfectly
in the still eye
        of the lake.

Who was it who
        threw the stone
from the pathway,
      f r a c t u r e d
    the image
      mirror – who?

Before all-smoothing Time
could restore
      a calm picture
of the shore
      wedded
        to the lake,
a breeze ruffled
      the surface.

THE PROMISE

I exit the world of black oak woods
where the last hour's drizzle filters down
from tired leaves to a sponge of moss.

I turn toward the shore, where the late
September rain is over. In sand, I leave
a trail of fresh-cut footprints where

other prints have mostly washed away.
Above my thoughts a pair of seagulls draw
imaginary lines that aren't quite parallel.

Above the gulls the clouds move on dark
wings to bless other woods, touch farther
shores, leave their redundant wetness

on the pocked face of distant waters.
My eyes are pulled to one fragile sail
rocking far too far off shore, pressing

stubbornly westward into the wind.
Raw gusts scratch my face as my feet
scuff on, ever nearer the lap of the water.

Where a wandering creek finds its lake,
I'm finally out of yesterday's office.
I've left Fidelity Trust. I'm away

from the fax and the water cooler, past
bobbing white buoys. The chill bites
through my jacket – how late is it?

My steps turn toward steaming lentil soup,
to the warm of her eyes and her arms –
to a promise made in the morning.

JUST SAY "NO!"

Told "no" again, again, we learn to say
our "no's" in pouting, spite, harsh bigotry,
as we progress from chilhood's mimicry
of "a-ah's," youthful "nah's," to voting "nay."

And yet we find it hard to take a stand
against cholesterol, salt, sweets and fat,
against tobacco, booze, small capsules that
can pump us up or calm the shaking hand.

Perhaps we've never learned to say a "yes"
with passion that would make our dull lives glow.
Avoiding evil, we bring up our score
to zero, full of sheer self-righteousness,
cold lovelessness. If all we know is "no,"
we focus on the wall and miss the door.

Poetry Titles Available from Chimney Hill Press

Edward Byrne –
Words Spoken, Words Unspoken
Bernhard Hillila –
a fly on the swatter
Cutting Edge